ADVENTURES IN NATURE

GARDEN FLOWERS

Cath Senker

PowerKiDS press™

Published in 2016 by
The Rosen Publishing Group, Inc.
29 East 21st Street, New York, NY 10010

Cataloging-in-Publication Data
Senker, Cath.
Garden flowers / by Cath Senker.
p. cm. — (Adventures in nature)
Includes index.
ISBN 978-1-5081-4583-7 (pbk.)
ISBN 978-1-5081-4584-4 (6-pack)
ISBN 978-1-5081-4585-1 (library binding)
1. Flowers — Juvenile literature.
2. Flowers — Identification — Juvenile literature.
I. Senker, Cath. II. Title.
QK49.S46 2016
582.13—d23

Copyright © 2016 Watts/PowerKids

Series Editor: Sarah Peutrill
Series Designer: Matt Lilly
Picture Researcher: Kathy Lockley
Illustrations: Andy Elkerton

Picture Credits: Alamy /R.Ann Kautzky 13c; Dreamstime.
com/Adam Radosavljevic 21CR, Adisa 8R, Alexander Potapov
7a, Annette Linnea Rasmussen 21RC, Anphotos 15(1), Brett
Critchley 21TC, ctpaul 7e, Dennis Van De Water 26B, 27BR, Dima
Smaglov 24B, Elena Luria 12, Filipe Varela 29a, Iona Grecu 15,
19BR, Jane Fedoseeva 6B, Jillmech 29c, Joerg Sinn 27BL, John
Pavel 20TR, Jurga Basinskaite 15, 19TL, Kai Xiao 20TL, Krzysztof
Korolonek 5TR, 15, Marilyn Barbone 22, Mark Brazier 10TR,
Maxximmm 18TR, 19ACR, Monika Adamczyk 28T, Naturablichter
15b, 19CR, Photka 29b, Richard Thomas 29BR, Sheryl Caston
23TR, Teena137 28B, Tr3gi 2, 10C, 12C,14BR,15(3),18BR, 23TC,
29BL, Volgariver 25TR, Waiheng 15a, Zhanghaobeibei 21C;
FLPA/dbn/Imagebroker 15(4); Shutterstock.com/Alexander
Mazurkevich 23LC, alybaba 13TR, Andriy Solovyov 13c, Anest 9e,
apiguide 8L, BestPhotoPlus 4T, BlueRingMedia 11T, c12 17TR,
CSLD 7bTC, Daimond Shutter 17TL, David Huntley Creative
26T, de2marco 14T, Debu55y 16BL, 19TR, Diana Talium 23TL,
Ian Grainger 13a, iLightphoto Contents page T, In Tune 9g,
irin-k 27TR, Isuaneye 16BR, J. Waldron 9f, Julia Sudnitskaya 5b,
LanKS 6T, Lapis2380 13b, Malgorzata Litkowska 10BL, Mariusz
S. Jurgielwicz 27RC, Mariyana M 9b, 21TLC, Martin Fowler
15(2), 23TC, Mizina Oksana 27TL, Moolkum 18B, NicO_I 9a,
nop16 27BC, Pakhnyuschchy 21R, patarpon attaporn 7c, Paula
Fisher 4B, Peangdao 7d, PHB.cz(Richard Semik) 23RAC, pjhpix
7f, Popoudina Svetlana 16C, PRILL 15(5), ra3m 13TL, rhfletcher
14B, romakova 28B(bckg), Roman Tsubin 27C, RubinowaDama
16TR, 19LC, Sandra Voogt 16TL, Sarah2 20BL, Shutova Elena
16LC, 21BR, Somchai rakin 11B, 30, Tamara Kulikova 9c, Tania
Zbrodko 7BL, taurus15 18LC, tratong Front Cover, TRL 23BL,
ueuaphoto 23BR, V.J.Matthew 24T, Vandycan 5c, Vilor Contents
page B5a, 21L, Wasanajai 23C, wavebreakmedia 29d; Wikipedia:
Tropaeolum majus, gouache on vellum, in Gottorfer Codex,
1649-59 by Hans-Simon Holtzbecker 9d

Manufactured in the United States of America

CPSIA Compliance Information: Batch #BW16PK: For Further Information contact
Rosen Publishing, New York, New York at 1-800-237-9932

Can you find SIX little forget-me-nots hidden on the pages?

Clara is out looking for GARDEN flowers. Can you find her?

There are lots more puzzles in this book. You can solve them by reading the text or by looking closely at the photos. The answers are on page 30.

Contents

flowers in the garden

It's fun to find out about the flowers in any garden.

Flowers come in all different sizes, shapes and colors. They can be huge – a sunflower is 12 inches (30 cm) wide, on a stem up to 13 feet (4 m) tall! Others are small, such as primroses, with delicate flowers just 1.2 inches (3 cm) across.

We grow flowers for their beautiful colors and to attract bees and butterflies and other helpful insects. We pick garden flowers to decorate our homes. Many flowers have a beautiful scent. They can be used to make perfume.

A flower bed full of beautiful small flowers.

This book will help you to hunt for flowers in the garden. Enjoy exploring but always check with an adult before touching or picking plants.

What is a flower?

A flower is the part of a plant that blossoms. Flowers make seeds that may turn into new plants. Most plants and many trees have flowers.

This primrose is flowering in spring.

Common garden flowers

What are these flowers called? Work out the anagrams to help you.

a

a s y p n

b

i u p n l

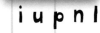

c

p l t u i

THE flower HUNT CHALLENGE

Find flowers

Find a garden where you can hunt for flowers: at home, school, or in your local park.

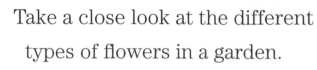

Flower petals

Take a close look at the different types of flowers in a garden. Many flowers are regular – the petals are all the same size and shape, forming a neat circle. Sweet-smelling roses and water lilies in ponds have regular flowers. Others, such as violets, are irregular – the petals are different shapes and sizes.

rose

Some blooms are made up of lots of little flowers that look like one large flower. Marigolds and asters are like this.

marigolds

Regular or irregular?

Which of these flowers are regular and which are irregular?

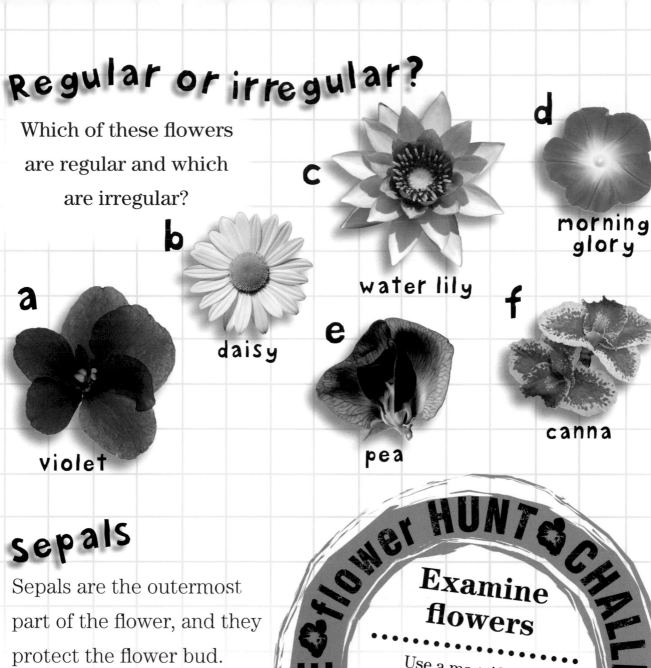

a violet

b daisy

c water lily

d morning glory

e pea

f canna

sepals

Sepals are the outermost part of the flower, and they protect the flower bud.

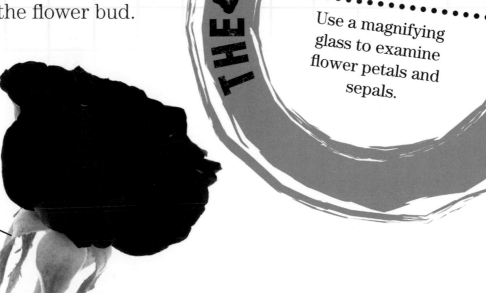

green sepals on a rose

THE flower HUNT CHALLENGE

Examine flowers

Use a magnifying glass to examine flower petals and sepals.

How do flowers grow?

To grow flowers, gardeners plant seeds they've bought from a garden center or saved from the previous year's flowers. To give the flowers a head start, they often plant them indoors or in a greenhouse during late winter or early spring. Seeds need warmth and water to begin to grow.

A gardener plants seedlings in a greenhouse.

An amaryllis, with its tall, sturdy stem, large bud, and flower.

First, the seed sends a root down into the soil, where it takes up water. The shoot pushes out of the soil into the air. The stem forms to support the leaves, which make food for the plant. Gardeners place their tiny seedlings in a light, sunny place where they grow bigger.

With regular watering, each plant grows tall and strong. The flower bud appears. Later, it opens, and the flower blossoms.

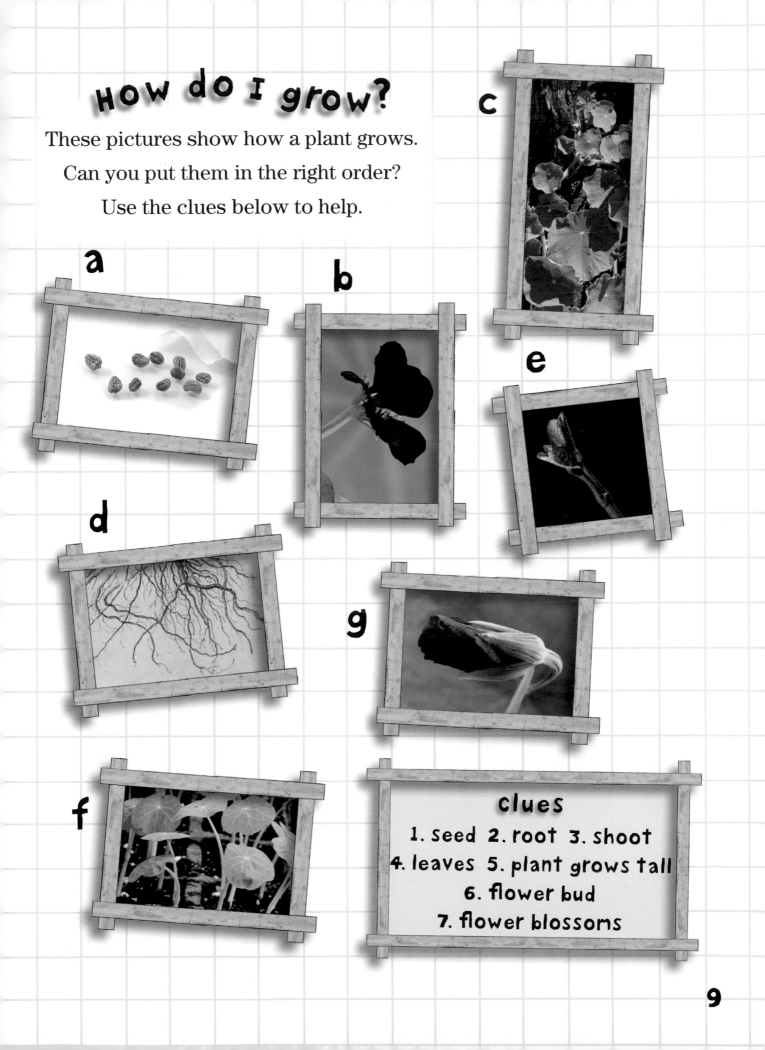

How do I grow?

These pictures show how a plant grows.

Can you put them in the right order?

Use the clues below to help.

a

b

c

d

e

f

g

clues
1. seed 2. root 3. shoot
4. leaves 5. plant grows tall
6. flower bud
7. flower blossoms

9

Pollination

When flowers appear, the plant is ready to reproduce. To do this, some plants need help from pollinating insects, especially bees and butterflies. Gardeners can grow their flying friends' favorite garden flowers to attract them.

A bee visits a flower to feed on nectar.

When a butterfly feeds on lavender nectar, it picks up pollen and takes it to the next flower.

In spring, bees flock to flowers such as bluebells and forget-me-nots to feed on pollen and nectar. In summer, bees and butterflies land on dahlias and marigolds. During late summer, heather and lavender have beautiful pink and mauve flowers that insects adore.

Male and female

Most flowers have male and female parts although some have one or the other. The stamen is the male part and makes pollen. The female carpel contains eggs. When a bee lands on a plant to feed, pollen sticks to its body. It flies to another plant of the same kind, where the pollen rubs off. The pollen fertilizes the eggs and makes seeds.

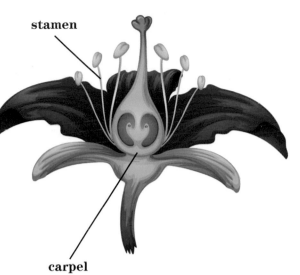

stamen

carpel

Spot the difference

Can you spot the four differences between these two pictures?

seed send-off

A seed is a tiny container with everything needed to make a new plant. Plants disperse their seeds so they won't grow right next to them and compete for light and water and food.

Some garden flowers disperse their seeds all by themselves – they are called self-seeding plants. They include honesty and California poppy. Gardeners plant them, they flower, the seeds fall around the garden, and they grow quickly into new plants.

Most garden flowers are spread by the wind. Seeds dispersed by wind are often light. Foxglove seeds are so light that they can float away on the breeze. Others, such as hosta seeds, have curved wings that catch easily in the wind.

The common foxglove self-seeds. This means that new seedlings spring up around the garden.

Flowers and seeds

Match the living
flower to the seed
head or pod.

hosta

clematis

sweet pea

a

b

c

THE flower HUNT CHALLENGE

Blow some seeds

Look out for dandelion
seed heads. One puff
and you can blow away
the seeds.

spring: the garden awakes

In spring, the garden wakes up after winter. The sun warms the soil, and the grass, flowering plants, and shrubs start to grow. It's a great time for the garden explorer!

Look closely at the soil. Snowdrops are often the first flowers to appear – their shoots can push through the snow in early spring, and little white flowers bloom. Other spring flowers such as pansies and primroses follow close behind.

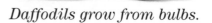

Daffodils grow from bulbs.

Many spring flowers come up each year, using energy stored in their bulbs underground. These include snowdrops, crocuses, and daffodils. A bulb is a winter plant stored under the ground that can grow into a new plant in spring.

Can you spot primroses, crocuses, and daffodils in this photo?

match the petals

Which flower does each petal belong to?

1

snowdrops

2

daffodils

3

primroses

crocuses

4

THE flower HUNT CHALLENGE

Signs of spring

Keep note of which plant flowers first in your garden. Which plant flowers next?

5

pansies

summer brightness

rose

Most flowers bloom during the long, hot days of summer. Look for these popular ones.

Roses have a lovely scent, but watch out for the thorns!

sunflower

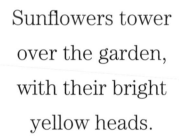

Sunflowers tower over the garden, with their bright yellow heads.

nasturtium

chrysanthemum

Chrysanthemums come in many colors. Look closely: each flower is made up of many tiny flowers called florets.

purple coneflower

fuchsia

In flower beds, look out for nasturtiums, coneflowers, and fuchsias, with their dangling flowers.

Splash of color

To provide a big splash of summer color, gardeners dig in bedding plants that are about to bloom. Impatiens, or busy lizzies, produce masses of pink, red and white flowers. Yellow and orange marigolds look cheerful and help to keep pests away.

impatiens

marigold

Flower puzzle

Can you identify these flowers from their outlines?

c

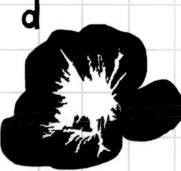

d

a

b

e

THE flower HUNT CHALLENGE

Press flowers

Ask if you can pick flowers. Put them between two layers of paper towels and then sheets of card stock. Place heavy books on top. Leave for a few weeks to flatten.

Autumn and winter color

In the autumn, the days grow shorter again. Summer flowers are busy producing seeds. Once they have released their seeds, they have done their job and they die – watch out for petals turning brown and falling off.

salvias

Some flowers bloom in autumn. Search for the spikes of pink, purple, or yellow flowers on salvias. (The herb sage is a salvia.) Hibiscus is a large shrub with dark green leaves. Its flowers have five or more petals and come in shades of red and yellow.

hibiscus

Pansies brighten up the winter garden.

Even in winter, some flowers can bloom, particularly in mild areas where the ground rarely freezes. You can plant pansies in the autumn to grow over winter into spring. Look for their five-petaled flowers – they often have little "faces."

seasonal flowers

Match the flower
to the season.
Remember: some
flowers bloom in more
than one season!

purple
coneflowers

pansies

spring
summer
autumn
winter

salvias

sunflowers

snowdrops

THE flower HUNT CHALLENGE

Seasonal photos

Take photos of the
garden in every season
to see how the flowers
come and go.

crocuses

Annuals, biennials, and perennials

peony

Why do some flowers come back each year but others die? See if you can spot these different kinds of garden flowers.

Perennials (from the Latin word meaning "many years") can survive all year round. They die back to the roots in winter and grow again in spring. Look out for peonies with their large round pink, white, and red flowers, and tall, pointed lupins in many colors.

love-in-a-mist

lupin

Annuals take just one year to grow from seeds, flower, release seeds and die. Gardeners plant them in spring for summer color. Check for nasturtiums and love-in-a-mist, with its layers of blue petals and fern-like leaves forming the "mist."

Biennials, such as foxglove, have a two-year life cycle – they flower in their second year. Foxgloves have tall spikes of bell-shaped flowers in purple, pink, and white.

what kind of flower am I?

Are these plants perennials, biennials, or annuals?

daffodils

snowdrops

rosemary

peonies

nasturtium

foxglove

21

The herb garden

Gardeners like to grow herbs – several kinds are perennials, growing year after year. They have a lovely scent, can be used in cooking and some have beautiful flowers in summer.

Some herbs grow all year round. In winter, look for soft, grey-green sage, spiky rosemary, and tiny thyme leaves. Throughout spring, rosemary and thyme have little pink, white, or purple flowers.

lavender

purple sage

rosemary

basil

thyme

golden thyme

sage

In summer, borage has beautiful blue flowers, each with five-pointed petals. Bees love them! Chamomile has daisy-like flowers with white petals and yellow centers. Chives have ball-shaped, purple flowers. The spiky leaves taste like onions.

match the flowers

Which flower belongs to which herb?

b

chamomile

thyme

c

d

a

borage

chives

THE flower HUNT CHALLENGE

Herb tasting

Rub some leaves from different herbs between your fingers to release the scent. Always check with an adult before you taste them!

Water flowers

If you're lucky enough to visit a garden pond, check for different flowers growing in and around it.

Be careful around water!

A garden pond filled with water lilies in flower.

Marginal plants create shade at the edge of the pond. Marsh marigolds are popular, with their large golden flowers in spring. Water forget-me-nots have clusters of little blue, white or yellow flowers, with white or yellow "eyes."

Water forget-me-nots grow easily by the edge of a pond.

Floating plants provide shelter for wildlife. They grow without being rooted to the bottom – their roots dangle in the water. Water hyacinths have a flower spike with striking light blue or violet flowers.

Some plants have leaves and flowers that float on the surface of the water while their roots stretch down to the bottom of the pond. Water lilies have floating flowers. Their wide, flat leaves spread the weight so they don't sink.

water lilies

Fill the pond

This little pond is empty. Where will each flower live?

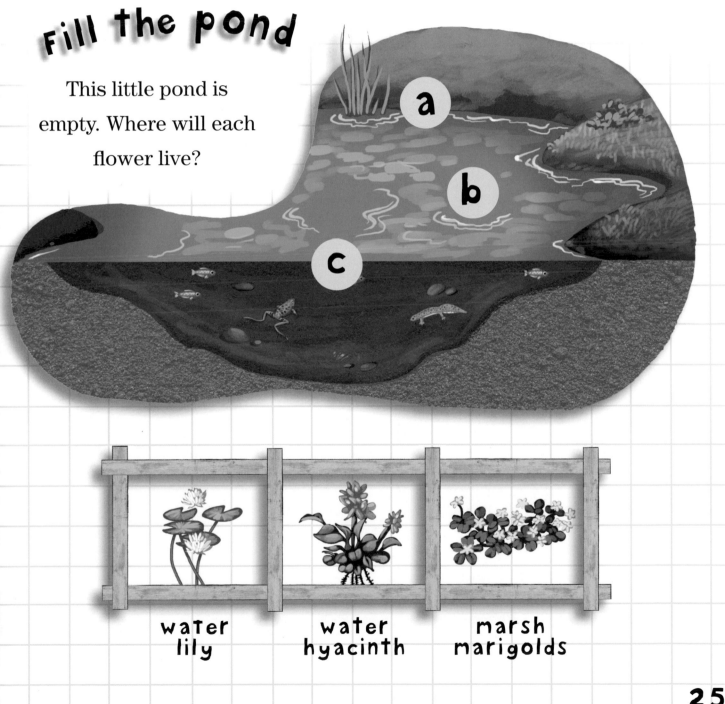

water lily

water hyacinth

marsh marigolds

War on weeds!

Gardeners are always complaining about weeds and trying to get rid of them. Weeds are plants that are growing where they're not wanted.

Why are they a problem? Weeds often grow fast. They compete with plants for water, light, and food from the soil. They produce lots of seeds, so they spread very quickly. And the seeds often survive for a long time.

Weeds grow anywhere – even between flowering plants.

On lawns, some flowering plants we call weeds look pretty and gardeners may choose to leave them. You may find delicate, yellow-centered white daisies, bright yellow buttercups, and many-petalled dandelions.

Dandelions and daisies are weeds but they're bright and cheerful.

weed or garden flower?

Look at these flowers. Which are weeds and which are popular garden flowers?

Dig them up

Gardeners dig up weeds using a hoe or trowel. Using weed killer can cause problems. Gardeners may damage their plants by mistake, and some chemicals harm bees and other helpful insects.

Make a mini flower garden

It's fun to grow flowers in the garden, or on a patio or windowsill.

Why not try these?

· Nasturtiums are pretty and you can eat the leaves and flowers in salads.

· Candy tuft flowers all summer.

· Pot marigolds and sunflowers are quick to grow.

· Sunflowers become extremely tall so make sure you have space!

A proud gardener!

Instructions

1 Pour soil mixed with compost into a large flower pot until it is three-quarters full.

2 Scatter the flower seeds. Sprinkle soil over the top and water well.

3 Put the pot in a warm, sunny place. Check it every couple of days and water the soil to keep it moist.

4 If the seeds come up squashed together, pull out the smallest ones.

5 Water your plants regularly and add fertilizer so they grow big and strong. Enjoy their flowers!

All in order

Can you put these steps for growing flowers in the right order? Use the steps below to help you.

a

e

b

d

c

1. Put some compost in a pot or spare bed.
2. Sprinkle the seeds and cover them with a thin layer of compost.
3. Water the pot regularly.
4. Watch out for your first seedlings.
5. Keep watering as your flowers grow.

Puzzle answers

5 Common garden flowers
a – pansy
b – lupin
c – tulip

7 Regular or irregular?
a – irregular
b – regular
c – regular
d – regular
e – irregular
f – irregular

9 How do I grow?
a, d, e, f, c, g, b

11 Spot the difference

13 Flowers and seeds
a – sweet pea
b – clematis
c – hosta

15 Match the petals
1 – pansies
2 – snowdrops
3 – primroses
4 – daffodils
5 – crocuses

17 Flower puzzle
a – sunflower
b – fuchsia
c – rose
d – nasturtium
e – purple coneflower

19 Seasonal flowers
purple coneflower –
summer
pansies – all seasons
salvias – autumn (also
summer)
sunflower – summer
snowdrops – winter/spring
crocuses – winter/spring

21 What kind of flower am I?
foxglove – biennial
snowdrop – perennial
daffodils – perennial
rosemary – perennial
peonies – perennial
nasturtium – annual

25 Fill the pond
a – marsh marigolds
b – water hyacinth
c – water lily

27 Weed or garden flower?
a – weed (daisy)
b – flower (rose)
c – flower (chamomile)
d – flower (sunflower)
e – weed (buttercup)
f – flower (marigold)
g – weed (dandelion)

23 Match the flowers
a – chamomile
b – thyme
c – chives
d – borage

29 All in order
c, b, e, a, d

Glossary

bedding plant A plant that is planted out in a garden bed, usually just before it flowers. It usually grows and dies within one year.

bloom To produce flowers.

blossom A flower or a mass of flowers, especially on a fruit tree or bush.

disperse To spread over a wide area.

fertilize Put pollen into a plant so that a seed develops.

flower bud A small lump that grows on a plant and from which a flower develops.

greenhouse A building with glass sides and a glass roof for growing plants in.

life cycle The series of forms into which a living thing changes as it develops.

mineral A substance that is found naturally in the earth, for example, salt.

nectar A sweet liquid that is produced by flowers and collected by bees for making honey.

pest An insect or animal that destroys plants and food.

pollen Fine powder, usually yellow, that is formed in flowers and carried to other flowers of the same kind by the wind or by insects, to make those flowers produce seeds.

pollination The process of pollen entering or being put into a flower or plant so that it produces seeds.

reproduce To produce young.

scent The pleasant smell that something has.

seedling A young plant that has grown from a seed.

sepal A part of a flower, like a leaf, that lies under and supports the petals.

shrub A large plant that is smaller than a tree and that has several stems of wood coming from the ground.

stem The main long, thin part of a plant above the ground from which the leaves or flowers grow.

thorn A small, sharp, pointed part on the stem of some plants, such as roses.

More ideas for flower hunts

To see a wide range of garden flowers, ask an adult to take you to a park, stately home, or a garden center. If you're really keen, you could visit special gardens that display beautiful flowers.

Index

A

annuals 20–21
autumn flowers 18–19

B

bees 4, 10, 27
biennials 20–21
bulbs 14
butterflies 4, 10

G

growing flowers 28–29

H

herbs 18, 22–23

P

parts of a flower 6–9, 11
perennials 20–22
petals 6–7, 15, 18, 22, 26
pollination 10–11
pond plants 6, 24–25

S

seeds 5, 8–9, 11–13, 18, 20, 26, 28–29
sepals 7
spring flowers 14–15, 22
summer flowers 16–18, 20–22

W

weeds 26–27
winter flowers 18–19

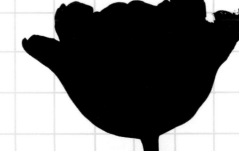

Websites

PowerKids Press has developed an online list of websites related to the subject of this book. This site is updated regularly. Please use this link to access the list:
www.powerkidslinks.com/ain/garden